I AM!!!

Book of Daily Affirmations

Crystal Foster

This book is dedicated to my mother, my children, and all of those who need to be reminded of who they are, those who need encouragement to becoming who they desire to be, and those who just are!

Make your next thought your next action and <u>BE</u>!!!

I AM THAT I AM
#iam

"I am!!!" A very powerful statement. You are declaring you are whatever you say you are. You are making a definitive statement that you are that which you desire to be, whether you are at this time in your life or not. And guess what? It's okay if you're not. Speak life into your livelihood. Then, follow up with action. This is how you **BECOME**!

Activity:
Make a list of all the things that describe you that are negative. Don't be afraid. You are not being judged. Examples of negative things that you may feel describe you are fearful, judgmental, obsessive, destructive, etc. Don't worry if you don't fill up all the lines…don't worry if you do.

Negative words that describe me.

Now take a moment to look up all the antonyms of each word. As you find each opposite, cross out each negative word. Hopefully, this will be the last time you describe yourself as such. Write the antonym on the table below after the words, "I am".

If you didn't have any negatives, don't worry. Just write down characteristics you aspire to have.

Antonyms of negative words that describe me or words I aspire to be.

These are the words you will focus on throughout this book. Every moment you exist should be a conscious effort to be the words above, until you become them and they become you. **I am that I am!**

Look at this list daily to remind you of who you are, to keep focus on being a better you, and to accomplish your goals. Say each statement daily (preferably in front of a mirror while looking at yourself) to reaffirm your "I am" statement.

Focus on one "I am" daily and put effort forth to be. Don't worry if you mess up. Just get yourself together by trying again. One step at a time. One day at a time.

Remember...if you are trying, you are doing. It may not be your best, but you are doing! That's what counts. Focus on the positive "I am" statements.

I AM = Thoughts Meeting Actions
#iam

"I am!!!" It is very important to understand that this statement is a product of your thoughts put into actions. You can say, "I am a mechanic," but if you're not <u>doing</u> any mechanic work, then you are not a mechanic.

To make a statement using "I am" requires actions. There are no ifs, ands, or buts about it.

"I am" is the sum of what you **DO**. Not of what you think. Not of what you say. It is solely based on your actions.

This book will require you to take action, not very much, but action nonetheless. The goal is to not only change your thoughts, but change what you do in relation to them. Don't just think it. Do it!

Remember, you are your actions. Say it. "I am my actions!" One more time, but a little louder. "I AM MY ACTIONS!"

Also, as you change, some people may question you, referring to a version of you that you no longer desire to be. Let them know that version of you is who you *were*, and now you are whatever it is you choose to be.

Goal: Better than yesterday!

MOVEMENT
#iam

Say it: I am MOVEMENT!!!

Everything is movement. This is what it all breaks down to (movement). Make every moment a movement...movement towards the things you want out of life. Movement to a better you. Movement to a better situation.

It's time to move in a manner that reflects the person you wish to be and the things you wish to have.

In which direction are you moving? Towards your goals? Towards your happiness? Towards your peace? Focus. Continue moving forward.

Activity:

Take a moment to think about your goals. Pick 3 goals: one that you would like to accomplish tomorrow, one for this week, and one that you would like to accomplish over the course of the next 30 days.

Write them down below and list one thing you can do to accomplish it in the "Action" field. Every day you should try to make a conscious decision to take actions to accomplish your goals.

As you accomplish them, put a check mark under the "Completed" column in the appropriate box.

	Goal	Action	Completed
Tomorrow Date: _____			
This week Date: _____			
Within 30 days Date: _____			

Day 2
PROGRESS
#iam

Say it: I am PROGRESS!!!

It is important that as you move, you are constantly progressing. Think about it. Your car can run, but it doesn't start moving until it is out of park. If it is not in park, you can easily move forward or backwards, depending on the direction you choose.

This is how you can look at your life and the people and things in it. Get some momentum and push forward towards accomplishing your goals, building your confidence, and becoming.

The act of choosing is important, but what matters just as much is what you choose to do. Make better choices. Participate in things that support your vision. Progress to become or have that which you seek.

Activity:
Before you take your car out of park, look in the rearview mirror and say, "I am progress! I am moving in the direction of my goals."

Make **conscious efforts** to think progressively.

Also, review your list of "I am" statements. Say them out loud and confidently because YOU ARE! I AM!

Day 3
ELEVATION
#iam

Say it: I am ELEVATION!!!

It is imperative that you always choose up. Being a better you requires you to make choices; better choices than you have made in the past. You are growing and that growth requires you to demonstrate this via actions.

Choose the high road. Choose to vibrate on a higher, stronger frequency. Choose to be above the situation. Elevate your mind. Elevate your actions.

Activity:
Think about the last time you had a "not so good" experience with someone. How could you have responded differently to the situation? How has this situation prepared you in the event you experience another situation similar to this?

_____

_____

_____

_____

_____

_____

_____

_____

The only person you can control is yourself. Take every opportunity to elevate your thought process and your actions.

Don't forget to keep track of your progress for this week's goal. Have you been working on it. If not, today is a perfect day to start. As the saying goes, "Don't put off tomorrow what you can do today." Tomorrow is not promised.

Also, review your "I am" statements. This is a daily activity. So, let's get to it!

LOYALTY
#iam

Say it: I am LOYALTY!!!

Loyal: giving or showing constant to something or someone.

Loyalty: the quality of being loyal.

Don't just practice being loyal. BE loyalty. More importantly, know **WHO** to be loyal to and **WHEN** to be loyal.

Often times we find ourselves being loyal to others before showing loyalty to ourselves. Don't sacrifice who you are just to appease the next person. Stand firm and be loyal. Sometimes, you must choose you. And guess what? This is 100% okay.

You are living your life. Be considerate of others, but know where your loyalty lies.

Activity:
Who/what are some people/things that you have a loyalty to? Does your loyalty to these things affect your wellbeing in a positive way? Are there things that you are loyal to that are toxic to your life and counterproductive to your goal?

These are very important questions to ask yourself. In the table on the next page write down things that you are loyal to that do not benefit you or they are toxic to you. Determine if you are going to continue to be loyal to these things. If yes, write down why. If not, write down what your course of action will be to separate yourself from it.

Remain loyal to saying your "I am" statements. That kind of slid right on in there. ☺

The Loyalty Box

Things I am loyal to that do NOT benefit me or is toxic to my life.	Am I going to continue to be loyal? (Yes/No)	If yes, then why? If no, how will I separate myself?

GRATEFUL
#iam

Say it: I am GRATEFUL!!!

Some say, "Gratitude is the best attitude," and I agree. Be appreciative of the people and things in your life. Everything has a purpose. Let them be (and know when to let them go). Be thankful of yourself and all that you do to elevate yourself to the next level.

Even when things don't go quite as planned or they seem utterly impossible to deal with, be thankful for the experience. Next time, if there is a next time, you will know how to handle the situation. Be thankful for the opportunity to learn and grow.

Activity:
Tell the world about something you are thankful for. Make a post on your favorite social media platform expressing gratitude for at least 3 things in your life. They can be anything, good or bad.

If it is bad, explain why you are grateful and how the situation pushed you to grow further in your journey. You're not doing this for likes. Be someone's inspiration today. You never know who is going through something similar and how your journey will affect theirs.

Have you said your "I am" statements today???

Day 6
WORTH
#iam

Say it: I am WORTH!!!

You are not just worthy, YOU ARE <u>WORTH</u>! The mere fact that you exist says to me that you are worth. Your very essence is valuable, if to no one else, to yourself. You are worth it! You are worthy! You are important! You are enough! You are deserving!

Activity:
The question is how much are you worth to **you**? How much time and effort are you spending on you to maintain and/or increase your self-worth? Spend more time building you up.

List some reasons why you are worth it. If you cannot think of anything, ask someone to help you out by asking them to tell you 2 things they like or admire about you.

REASONS WHY I AM WORTH IT

Affirmation time! Review your "I am" statements.

GROWTH
#iam

Say it: I am GROWTH!!!

You are more knowledgeable. You are stronger. You are wiser. You are taking more action. You are more today than you were yesterday. You have grown.

You are making decisions that promote your growth. Whether you are looking for your roots or branches to become longer and/or stronger, you are definitely making progress.

You are more conscious. You are more aware. You are maturing and blossoming.

Activity:
It has been 7 days since you started this journey. Did you accomplish your week's goal set on Day 1?

If you answered yes, what was the most difficult part of accomplishing the goal? If you had to redo it, what would you do differently and why or why not?

_____
_____
_____
_____
_____
_____
_____

If your answer is no, what held you back? What can you do this upcoming week to change the outcome?

_____
_____
_____
_____
_____
_____
_____
_____

Review your "I am" statements!

Day 8
OPEN
#iam

Say it: I am OPEN!!!

You are open!!! You are open to receiving abundance. You are open to new ideas and opportunities. There's more than one way to skin a cat! And you are open to learning and being more efficient.

You are open to all of the success that is coming your way. You are open to new ways to accomplishing your goals. You are open to receiving positive feedback and turning criticism in additional ways to critique your plan.

You are choosing to go through life with an open mind and open heart.

Activity:
Take a moment to think about a time someone "hated" on you (made a negative statement about you). What did they say? How did that make you feel? Was there any validity to their statement? If they would have said what they said differently, in a more positive light, would you have received the message differently? How can you take what was said and make it work to your benefit?

_____
_____
_____
_____
_____
_____
_____
_____
_____
_____
_____
_____

It is important that you open yourself up to receive feedback and learn how to turn negative feedback into a positive. If you find yourself in a situation where someone is shining light on a negative situation, figure out how to flip the situation and/or obtain resolution.

Have you heard yourself say your "I am" statements today?

AMBITION
#iam

Say it: I am AMBITION!!!

You are determined...determined to accomplish being the best you there is!

You are driven...driven to move in the direction that supports your vision.

You are a goalsetter and a goal-smasher.

You are achieving. You are passionate. You take initiative (by obtaining a copy of this book, for example). You are intentional with your actions. You move with purpose and you're hungry for success.

Activity:
Think of the last time you felt ambitious. Write down how that felt to you.

Did you accomplish what you sought out to do? Why or why not? If so, is there anything you would have done differently? If not, what can you do differently to move to the next step?

_____
_____
_____
_____
_____
_____
_____
_____
_____
_____
_____
_____
_____
_____
_____

Check out your "I am" statements!!!

CONFIDENT
#iam

Say it: I am CONFIDENT!!!

You are making confident and conscious decisions to be the best you and accomplish your goals. You are absolutely and positively making choices that are aligned with your dreams. You are holding your head high as you walk down your path. You are certain that your actions support your vision.

Activity:
Do an internet search on power colors. Choose a color that represents a feeling you'd like to convey. Then, wear a shirt with that color. Style your hair and/or groom your beard.

Look yourself in the mirror and sell yourself to yourself. Tell yourself why you are great. If you don't know, revisit your "I am" statements. Speak firmly. Speak loudly. Speak!!!

Next, compliment 3 people on things that they **do**, not their looks, and smile. Embody confidence and exchange the energy.

How did that make you feel?

_____
_____
_____
_____
_____
_____
_____
_____

...review your "I am" statements.

KNOWLEDGE
#iam

Say it: I am KNOWLEDGE!!!

You are self-aware and know yourself better than anyone else. You are educated. You are intelligent. You make smart and strategic moves.

You are learning what you need to know to be a better you than yesterday. You are studying information that betters your vision. You are experiencing things that only your journey of movement could teach you. You know better, so you **DO** better.

You are wisdom. You are intellect. You are enlightened. You are understanding. Your actions prove that you are these things.

Activity:
When was the last time you did some research on your goal or an area of your character that you struggle with. Today, go look up some information that can be applied to your daily thought process and your daily actions that supports your vision of who you want to become or what you want to have.

Name one new thing you can do to accomplish your goals?

_____
_____
_____
_____
_____
_____
_____
_____
_____
_____
_____
_____
_____
_____
_____
_____

RESPONSIVE
#iam

Say it: I am RESPONSIVE!!!

You are positive reactions. You are in control of your reactions. You are responding and doing so with calculated moves. You are deliberately taking steps with your goal in sight.

You are creating a call to action and moving your feet. You are answering your call to vibrate on a higher level. You are conducting yourself in a manner that supports your vision.

You are responding with actions. You are responding to great opportunities.You are responsive!!!

Activity:
Review your "I am" statements. Choose one and use it in a conversation today. You are going to be engaging.

Create a post on social media with your "I am" statement and ask people how they are doing. Respond to at least your first 3 likes (not just your comments, but likes) by asking people how they are doing or **what** they are doing or what are their goals.

How did this make you feel?

_____
_____
_____
_____
_____
_____
_____
_____
_____

Are you becoming? Check out your "I am" statements and evaluate your progress.

FIERCE
#iam

Say it: I am FIERCE!!!

You are powerful and making power moves. You are going toe to toe with fear and WINNING!!! You are strong. You are passionate. You have a swag like no other.

You are taking control of your destiny. You understand that the wavelength you vibe on is forceful, moving things into alignment with your goals and aspirations. You are relentless in ensuring you knock out some of your goals.

Activity:
Revisit the "Loyalty" activity. Have you completed the process of cutting ties? If not, why? Whether you did or didn't, have you noticed any changes with how you are handling people in regards to how they handle you?

_____
_____
_____
_____
_____
_____
_____
_____
_____
_____
_____
_____
_____
_____
_____
_____

Revisit your "I am" statements.

Day 14
ACCEPTING
#iam

Say it: I am ACCEPTING!!!

You are giving yourself express consent to accept everything positive that comes your way. You are acquiring the wherewithal to motivate yourself to accomplishing your goals. You are obtaining the things that you desire to have.

You are accepting the change that is here and that will be coming your way. You are accepting the growth that you are experiencing. You are expressing acceptance to what is and moving your feet in the direction that you choose.

Activity:
Here are a few things to think about:

What is one thing in your life that you have a hard time accepting? Is the fact that you are not accepting "what is" holding you back in any way shape or form? Do you spend unnecessary time thinking about what could have happened or what should have happened? What can you do to move past these types of thoughts?

_____
_____
_____
_____
_____
_____
_____
_____
_____
_____
_____
_____
_____
_____
_____
_____
_____

If you are not going to do something about it, let it go. If you are going to do something about it, plan it out and do it...just like your "I am" statements (Hint: this is another reminder).

Day 15
PRODUCTIVE
#iam

Say it: I am PRODUCTIVE!!!

You are moving with purpose. You are working to compose a life of abundance. You are bringing the best of you out into the world. You are producing wondrous vibrations that are attracting that which you desire to be and have into your life.

You are walking in your path. You are having meaningful conversations that support your dreams. You are industrious; working hard to accomplish your goals.

Your mind is fertile and fruitful, producing positive thoughts to make your vision a reality. You are productive!

Activity:
What motivates you? It's time to sit down and think about the things that move your spirit. Take a moment to reflect on the times where you appeared to be stagnant and stuck. What are some of the things you did to revitalize yourself? What advice would you give your younger self to help get your feet moving?

_____
_____
_____
_____
_____
_____
_____
_____
_____
_____
_____
_____
_____
_____
_____
_____

Don't forget about your "I am" statements. If you find yourself unable to remember to do them, take a moment to write them down and post them in your bedroom, on the mirror, in your car, etc. to help reinforce that which you desire to have or become. Manifest it.

ADAPTATION
#iam

Say it: I am ADAPTATION!!!

You are reshaping your life to be what you desire it to be. You are changing your actions to be aligned with your thoughts. You are altering your thoughts to be more positive and supportive of YOU!

You are reconstructing every notion of yourself that you are not content with. You are going through a metamorphosis and turning into a beautiful version of your most beautiful self. You are adapting to the positive energy that is flowing through your life.

You are metamorphosis. You are transformation. You are change.
You are adapting to things that require you to change in order to fulfill your purpose.

Activity:
Change can be stressful. Take a moment to think about the following questions. Create yourself a road map on how to handle change.

What are some of your ways you decompress? Do you find yourself complaining more often than not? What are some of the things you complain about? Is it worth your time and effort to speak on those situations? Why or why not? What can YOU do to resolve the issue? If nothing, what can you do to change your perception of the situation.

_____
_____
_____
_____
_____
_____
_____
_____
_____

I see you saying your "I am" statements in the near future. LOL

AWARE
#iam

Say it: I am AWARE!!!

You are aware of the positive changes that are taking place in your life. You are cognizant of the things that need to take place in order for you to achieve your goal. You are knowledgeable about the topics surrounding your goal and are using the information to your benefit.

You are well-informed. You realize that your goals are achievable and you are doing what it takes to accomplish them. You know what's going on and you are mindful of your actions.

Activity:
Simple task: Take a moment and observe your scenery. Do a little people or nature watching for a few minutes. Did you notice anything today that you hadn't noticed before? Did you find some level of focus and peace? Why or why not?

_____
_____
_____
_____
_____
_____
_____
_____
_____
_____
_____
_____
_____
_____
_____
_____

I am here to tell you that YOU ARE!!! You are everything you desire to be. Just go recite those "I am" statements and listen to yourself validate what I said. Make sure your actions are following suit.

PROACTIVE
#iam

Say it: I am PROACTIVE!!!

You are taking charge!!! Your thoughts and actions are a catalyst to accomplishing your goals. You are conscious and strategically moving in directions that support your vision.

You are making decisions that will counter any issues that arise and using them as lessons to further your growth. You are attentive and correcting mistakes as or before they happen. You are working through possible obstacles and objections before they arise. You are piloting your own plane!

Activity:
Do you find yourself overwhelmed at times? You have a plan, but don't know where to start. Or maybe you know how to start and how to finish, it's just getting things accomplished or completed that's holding you back? Where does time go? *le sigh*

Take a moment to prioritize your tasks and delegate simple things to others, if possible. Then, move your feet and get the tasks completed. Don't be afraid to ask for help either.

Priorities:

Duties to Delegate:

Let's work smarter (like saying those "I am" statements) not harder.

COURAGEOUS
#iam

Say it: I am COURAGEOUS!!!

You are brave! You are overcoming your self-doubt. You are treading through the difficulties of accomplishing your goals and succeeding.

You understand that the real courage was walking down your path to accomplish your goals. It was in the steps it took and takes to get and keep the ball moving.

The more steps you take, the more fearless you become. Everything becomes part of the process and you are boldly taking on whatever comes your way, utilizing the tools you have acquired to help you.

Activity:
Think about the last time you were afraid to do something, but did it anyway. Why were you afraid? Was it rational fear? How did you overcome it? Can the same method you used to overcome this fear help you with something in relation to your current goals?

_____
_____
_____
_____
_____
_____
_____
_____
_____
_____
_____
_____
_____
_____
_____
_____

Don't be afraid to say your "I am" statements out loud. Continue speaking them into existence.

OPTIMISTIC
#iam

Say it: I am OPTIMISTIC!!!

NO MORE PESSIMISM! You are what you think! You are what you do!

You have a fresh outlook on life. You know why? Because you are making decisions that support your vision. You are hopeful. You are undoubting. You are confident. Even through your trials, you are anticipating your triumphs, keeping your eye on the prize.

You are auspicious and everything you do is conducive to the success of your goals. You are positive. You are not just shining, you are glowing because you are the light!!! You are the light!

Activity:
If you are already not positive, you have got to change the way you think. Yes, there is always the possibility that something will not go as planned. However, there is also a possibility that everything will be just right or even better. So accept the fact that either could happen, even when the possibility of one happening over the other is greater...or always shoot for the best. Why not?! What do you have to lose?

Oh, so you're afraid to be disappointed or you just don't want to be disappointed. That's understandable, but if you have accepted that as a possibility, why not go for it? The more you take strides to go after that which you seek rather than be lead by possible disappointment, despair, loss, etc., the easier things will become. Well, at least the option to chose things that support your vision will. Keep the faith and keep moving your feet.

Practice asking questions that you feel you know the answer to will be no. You will be pleasantly surprised when someone responds to at least one with a yes. It is better to hear the "no" and know, than to guess that will be the answer and never truly know. But can you imagine how much better you feel when you will hear that "yes"?

Did you say your "I am" statements? YES! Yes, you did or yes, you will. I love hearing that!!! You make me so proud.

Day 21
EARNEST
#iam

Say it: I am EARNEST!!!

You are serious about achieving your goals. You are determined and committed to seeing it through. Everyday you are making an effort to make your vision a reality.

You are diligent in your pursuit of being a better you and ensuring your goals are being met. You are consistently navigating in the direction of your goals. You are dedicated to seeing your dreams come true. You not only know that your thoughts are important, but so are your actions, and you are serious about getting things done.

Activity:
Today, take an opportunity to reflect on previous activities. It's one thing to live it and it's another to observe it. Observe to understand and see your growth. Retrospection Kings and Queens!

Now, where art thou "I am" statements? Let's get it, shall we?!

UNWAVERING
#iam

Say it: I am UNWAVERING!!!

No matter how you look at it, you are thriving. You are keeping consistency as you move to obtain your dreams. You are steadfast with your options to choose better things for a better situation.

You are dedicated to achieving your goal. You are determined. You are relentless in your efforts to accomplishing your dreams. This is unwavering. This is what you are.

Activity:
Stay committed! You ARE, so continue to be. Today, say your "I am" statements 3 times. Make time and execute with conviction. Believe what you say and keep your word...if to no one else, honor <u>yourself</u> by keeping your word to you. Just be all of those things. Be that which you are. You don't owe it to anyone, but you!

DISCERNMENT
#iam

Say it: I am DISCERNMENT!!!

You are recognizing things that support your goals. You are working to create moves that help make your mental vision a physical reality. You are understanding the difference between what does and does not serve you.

You are seeking peace and finding it with each choice you make. You electing to vibrate on a different frequency, attracting great vibes that strengthen yours. You are deciding to choose things that enhance your wisdom. You are perceiving every possible moment as a moment to better yourself and reach your dreams.

Activity:
Time to revisit Day 4's activity. If you have successful cut out toxic people and things in your life, then great! Today will be an easy day of reflection. If you have not, then it is time to practice discernment and make some serious decisions.

"I am" statements, please and thank you.

INNOVATIVE
#iam

Say it: I am INNOVATIVE!!!

You are creative. You are fresh and original. Let's face it, there's only one you. You are establishing the groundwork for your goals you are accomplishing. You are asking the right questions and aligning them with the correct solutions.

You are creating a pathway for your continued success. You are introducing your mind to new concepts that you're applying to your daily lifestyle. You are innovation in it's finest form because you are you!

Activity:
When was the last time you created something? Take a moment to do an arts and crafts activity or write a story or poem. Give yourself at the very least 5 minutes. Get those creative juices flowing. Make time to inspire yourself.

While you're creating, say your "I am" statements.

Day 25
CLARITY
#iam

Say it: I am CLARITY!!!

You are clarity. Your heart and mind are seeing with a new pair of eyes causing you to continuously choose that which supports your visions. Your mind is clear and you are focused. You easily move past and overcome obstacles because you can foresee how they affect your dreams. You understand what it takes to win and you are choosing the path of success.

Activity:
Day 25 and you're alive! Yas! I can see clearly now the rain is gone. Since starting your journey, what things have you perceived differently? What have been some eye opening situations that have taken place where you initially thought one way, but has now your outlook on the situation or thing has changed?

_____
_____
_____
_____
_____
_____
_____
_____
_____
_____
_____
_____
_____
_____
_____
_____

Make sure you clearly state those "I am" statements.

EFFICIENT
#iam

Say it: I am EFFICIENT!!!

You are focused. You are productive. Your decisions are effective and benefit your overall goals.

You are strategically planning. You move methodically to ensure your reality mirrors or excels that which you have envisioned. You are well-organized and make logical decisions that support your vision.

Activity:
How often do you plan and prioritize? Time to reassess your actions to ensure they are aligned with your goals. Can you adjust areas in your life to be more productive and/or save time?

What are some things that you can rearrange in your life so that you have more time to pursue your dream? Are certain things necessary? Are there any opportunities that may arise that you foresee? How can you prepare yourself for those things and, most importantly, when can preparation be complete?

Take a moment to document things so that you can gain perspective.

_____
_____
_____
_____
_____
_____
_____
_____
_____
_____
_____
_____
_____

Also, don't forget about your "I am" statements.

Day 27
POSITIVE
#iam

Say it: I am POSITIVE!!!
You choose to see the bright side of things. You know that the great energy you are putting out in the universe is attracting more great energy. You are optimistic.

Your actions are supportive of your goals. You possess the qualities to accomplish your dreams and are using them to make them a reality. You are putting forth the effort needed to complete your tasks at hand. You are attracting what you are putting out...GREAT ENERGY!

Activity:
It is important for you to continue to think positively. This week, take a moment to observe your thoughts and actions. Are you primarily positive? What were some things that triggered negative thoughts?

_____
_____
_____
_____
_____
_____
_____
_____

What are some things you can do once those thoughts appear? Develop a strategy or thought replacement therapy moment to get you back on track when you find your mind in a negative space. Begin to put that strategy in place. Remember, you want to think progressively. Your actions should follow suit.

_____
_____
_____
_____
_____
_____
_____

Say those "I am" statements with conviction and believe.

COMMUNICATIVE
#iam

Say it: I am COMMUNICATIVE!!!

You are expressing your needs. You are letting others and the universe know what it is you are looking for. You are attracting what you want because you are articulating your desires.

You use warm and welcoming body language to build rapport while networking. You are conveying your feelings. You are confident with your words. You are articulate. You are expression.

Activity:
Looking at your "I am" statements, are there things that you are still struggling with? If so, time to dig deeper. Why do you feel that way?

_____
_____
_____
_____
_____
_____
_____
_____
_____

What are some things that have happened that makes you think otherwise? What can you do about it? How can you accept what is and move on? What would you say if you had to provide advice to a friend going through your same struggle?

_____
_____
_____
_____
_____
_____
_____
_____
_____

Sometimes you have to communicate with yourself. Listen to yourself. Seek within and be attentive to you for a change. Express yourself. Preach to yourself and practice what you preach...like practicing those "I am" statements. Lol I'm just saying.

RESILIENT
#iam

Say it: I am RESILIENT!!!

You got that bounce back! You are a go-getter. You refuse to let things deter you from accomplishing your goals. Setbacks are your opportunities to reevaluate your vision and learn...and you do just that!

You spring to life as you approach and OVERCOME obstacles. You persevere through trials. You evaluate yourself when situations get you down. You are a second wind. You are dope like that!

Activity:
Sometimes it is necessary to understand that life moves like wavelengths. There are highs. There are lows. There are constant moments of descension and ascension. You must realize and accept that.

Sometimes a decline is needed before the increase. You are to learn and prepare. When was the last time you had a down moment? What did it take for you to change that into an positive? How can you apply that same logic to your goals?

_____
_____
_____
_____
_____
_____
_____
_____
_____
_____
_____
_____
_____
_____
_____
_____

Look at you remembering those "I am" statements. Proud moment!

Day 30
SUCCESS
#iam

Say it: I am SUCCESS!!!

You are completion. You are accomplishment. You are victorious.

You are execution. You are admiration. You are inspiration. You are doing! You have BECOME!

Activity:
You have committed, followed through, and successfully completed this "I am" journey. I am so proud of you. You are proud of you. Make a post and feel free to tag me on how this book helped you. What did you learned about yourself? Did you truly apply yourself? Have you noticed any changes?

_____
_____
_____
_____
_____
_____
_____
_____
_____

Also, were you able to complete your 30 day goal? If so, it is time create a new one and plan out how to get it accomplished. If not, it is time to reevaluate your goal and your actions. Why aren't you committed and what can you do to change that? Anything is possible.

_____
_____
_____
_____
_____
_____
_____

Before we end this journey, please take one more moment (or as many as you want) to reflect and remind yourself of who you are, who you have become, and who you are striving to be (say those "I am" statements).

Thank you! You are unequivocally dope!!! Follow me on IG @iamcfoster1 for more inspirational, uplifting, thoughtful posts dedicated to inspiring and motivating you.

Made in the USA
Columbia, SC
24 May 2019